DEPRESSION
AND MUSIC

DEPRESSION AND MUSIC

Prelude to a historical theme

Published by
Organon International bv
Oss, The Netherlands, 1989

CIP-GEGEVENS KONINKLIJKE BIBLIOTHEEK, DEN HAAG

Lieburg, M.J. van

Depression and music : prelude to a historical theme /
[text: M.J. van Lieburg ; ed.: P. Verhoef ; transl. from
the Dutch by Stichting Tekstverzorging]. – Rotterdam :
Pharmad Publishing ; Oss : Organon International. – Ill.
– (A different view of depression ; 3)
Vert. van: Depressie en muziek. – Oss : Organon Nederland ;
Rotterdam : Pharmad Publishing, 1988. – Met lit. opg.
ISBN 90-5235-003-5 geb.
SISO 606.3 UDC [616.89+159.972]: 78
Trefw.: depressiviteit en muziek.

'Depression and Music' is the third volume of a series of cultural-historical sketches called 'A different view of depression', compiled on behalf of Organon International bv.

Already published:
1 Famous depressives, ten historical sketches, 1988
2 An unknown monograph on depressions, 1988

Text: Prof. Dr. M.J. van Lieburg
Erasmus University Rotterdam/Free University Amsterdam
Design and realization: Pharmad Publishing Rotterdam

Copyright 1989 Organon International bv, Oss, The Netherlands.
This book may not be reproduced in whole or in part and/or otherwise circulated by means of print, photocopy, microfilm or in any other form whatsoever without the publisher's prior written consent.

Reproduction rights to the illustrations are being sought in accordance with legal stipulations.

Contents

Preface	7
The magic-religious dimension of music therapy	9
Saul and David: depression and music in antiquity	10
Music therapy in Western culture	15
Hugo van der Goes	17
Medieval and early modern perceptions of music therapy	20
Music therapy and depression	25
Iatro-musica	27
Music and depression in the Age of Reason	31
Music therapy in the Age of Enlightenment	35
Carlo Broschi Farinelli	37
A Gallic view on melancholy	42
Depression and musical genius	45
Wolfgang Amadeus Mozart	47
Ludwig van Beethoven	51
Musical analysis of 'La Malinconia'	56
Depression and music in the 19th and 20th century	61
The scepticism of French psychiatry	63
A depressive quartet from 19th century music	67
Depression and music in the 20th century	73
Bibliography	75

Preface

In the historian's search for melancholy and depression in the history of music – even more so than in tracking down 'famous depressives' in general history (see volume 1 of this series) – he can actually do little more than what the renowned gold diggers did in the past: creep through the rubble and debris of historical data contained in published source material and extract those items whose promising glitter arouses his expectations. However, even in the historian's case not everything that glitters ultimately turns out to be gold, since in the melting furnace of historical critique very little is usually left over which lends itself to further consideration.

All this does not alter the fact that everything compiled in this edition about the musical facets of the history of depressive disorders can nevertheless give an impression of the age-long relationship between the depressive human being and music. Aside from the theoretical reflection of music on the human mind, this relationship also involves the therapeutic use of music in the treatment of depressive disorders and the expression in music of the human being's inner self dominated by melancholy feelings.

This historical account does not offer the definitive evaluation of current medical, musicological and historical views on the information and insights supplied by the sources with regard to the relationship between depression and music. It rather concerns a kaleidoscopic selection of a few high points and main features. Being able to use medical and music-historical literature already gathered was a great help in this case. The studies of Werner F. Kümmel and the review compiled by Jean Starobinski deserve special mention.

Many of the questions forcing themselves upon us from the history of the relationship between depressions and music are silently passed over in this treatise. As long as such questions are still raising so much discussion even today, one cannot expect a uniform answer or definitive solution from history. Depression and music are still surrounded by many mysteries! Both subjects belong to the areas of human knowledge which are still as fascinating as they are uncomprehended. This fascination and the awareness of being faced with an impenetrable reality can only be reinforced by an introduction to the past.

The magic-religious dimension of music therapy

Awareness of the fact that making music is far more than producing sound has already had an effect on the application of music in the world of religion and magic at an early stage. It is the ability to touch the inner self of a human being, his feelings, his emotions and moods to which music owes its place in our culture. Once man had discovered the affective value of music and its communicative qualities, a continuous search followed for new compositions of sound and tone, for new possibilities with regard to the mechanisms and design of all sorts of musical instruments, and for new interpretations of the musical achievements earlier produced by others.

All kinds of religious rituals surrounding gods and goddesses of old civilizations, and the magic-religious performance of the medicine man or shaman in various earlier and present non-Western cultures are thus inseparably connected with the use of music. Such rituals frequently acted and still act as the ceremonial expression of the medical treatment. This is undoubtedly a direct consequence of the conviction that the presence of physical and psychic disorders is determined by higher powers. Without the knowledge of the history of music and musicology of old civilizations and non-Western cultures, the study of archaic and ethnological medicine and psychiatry would be quite impossible.

Saul and David: depression and music in antiquity

The contents of the earliest historical sources and the older history of music therapy in the treatment of depressive disorders concentrate mainly on the biblical figures Saul and David, respectively the first King of Israel and his younger rival. Aside from the deeper, primarily religious significance of this story in Jewish and Christian thinking concerning the rise of the David dynasty, the episode in which a music-therapeutic relationship existed between both rivals was only a moderate part of the life stories of both men.

In the Old Testament's Book of Samuel, this episode is preceded by an account in which the author indicates how Saul became increasingly possessed by an evil spirit, while David manifested himself more and more clearly as the 'anointed' of Yahweh. In addition, it is recounted how David gradually grew more involved with the court of Saul: he became his armour-bearer, made friends with Saul's son Jonathan and later married Saul's daughter, Michal. Shortly after Samuel made it obvious to Saul that he could no longer count on Yahweh's favour, Saul manifested his mental illness in a most vehement manner.

It was in this situation that David was called to the court of Saul to help combat the demonic disease with his harp and lyre playing and perhaps also his song. It can be deduced from various reports that David was endowed with remarkable musical qualities. His play on the Israelite 'kinnor' and his singing must have impressed people around him since his childhood.

> *'Now the Spirit of the Lord departed from Saul, and an evil spirit from the Lord tormented him. And Saul's servants said to him, "Behold now, an evil spirit from God is tormenting you. Let our lord now command your servants, who are before*

David plays for Saul on the harp. Copperplate by Lucas van Leyden, 1509.

you, to seek out a man who is skilful in playing the lyre; and when the evil spirit from God is upon you, he will play it, and you will be well." So Saul said to his servants, "Provide for me a man who can play well, and bring him to me."
One of the young men answered, "Behold, I have seen a son of Jesse the Bethlehemite, who is skilful in playing, a man of valour, a man of war, prudent in speech, and a man of good presence; and the

Lord is with him." Therefore Saul sent messengers to Jesse and said, "Send me David your son, who is with the sheep." And Jesse took an ass laden with bread, and a skin of wine and a kid, and sent them by David his son to Saul. And David came to Saul, and entered his service. And Saul loved him greatly, and he became his armour-bearer. And Saul sent to Jesse, saying, "Let David remain in my service, for he has found favour in my sight." And whenever the evil spirit from God was upon Saul, David took the lyre and played it with his hand; so Saul was refreshed, and was well, and the evil spirit departed from him' (1 Samuel 16:14-23).

From the continuation of this story it is known that despite hopeful expectations of the effect of music therapy, Saul's illness apparently became increasingly more serious. Several chapters after it was first reported that David entered Saul's service as a music therapist, it is recounted how the evil spirit had seized Saul once again. '...and he raved within his house, while David was playing the lyre, as he did day by day. Saul had his spear in his hand; and Saul cast the spear, for he thought, I will pin David to the wall. But David evaded him twice' (1 Samuel 18:10-11; and also 19:9-10).

As far as factual history is concerned, Saul's illness calls for further explanation. Through the years, a great diversity of opinion has been aired about this subject. During the early stages of Christianity, Saul was considered the prototype of an apostate possessed by demons. Others, particularly from a later period, believed that it concerned a manic-depressive psychosis to which, as is known, the collective name of melancholy was usually assigned in the past.

With the help of several bible passages, it was possible to observe the gradual development of Saul's illness. For instance, the proverbial question "Is Saul also among the prophets?" supposedly points to an early emotional instability and an extreme susceptibility to psychic infection through group agitation. In addition, literature speaks of epilepsy and an 'anxietas praecordialis', which actually occurs primarily in melancholiacs. A rather divergent view was introduced in 1970 by Simon Levin, based on the mention in Saul's pathography of giantism, loss of peripheral vision and mental illness. According to Levin, this combination supposedly points in the direction of a hypophysis tumour. The music therapy was thus intended to reduce the consequently resulting headaches.

In his study about the story of David and Saul in both the history of music and medicine, Werner Kümmel shows how the interpretation of this story has been subject to all sorts of changes over the course of centuries. First of all, there was a difference of opinion regarding the question of whether Saul's disorder should be considered a mental illness determined by medical factors, or as a case of possession involving demonic powers. Since the 13th and 14th centuries, the conviction had taken root that in the first instance the illness could indeed be cured with the help of music. In the second case, it could not have constituted more than a means of alleviating the tormenting presence of the demon(s), or to make the stay in the body of the possessed less pleasant for the demon(s) as a result of the altered physical disposition brought on by the music.

In this line of thought, emphasis is consequently placed on the magic-religious effect which must have emanated from David's presence in general and his prayers and song in particular. After all, demons are spirits without an organ of hearing and without affects, and they won't let themselves be driven away by musical sounds; this can, however, be achieved by persons who are blessed with the spirit of Yahweh and radiate this in their religious songs through their charismatic presence.

David in the role of Saul's music therapist. Painting by Rembrandt, about 1655 (Mauritshuis, The Hague).

Furthermore, the view that it did not involve an instrumental but rather a vocal performance (incantation) by David was emphatically mentioned in the *Liber Antiquitatum Biblicarum* (1527) published by Pseudo-Philo which also reproduces the psalm that David was said to have rendered during his therapeutic sessions.

Finally, there is the flow of tears which was considered a part of the catharsis, the purifying process, initiated by the music. This phenomenon is also depicted in the painting which Rembrandt made of David playing the lyre at the court of Saul, and where Saul's deep depression can be read in his tear-stained face.

Music therapy in Western culture

The idea of a harmonious cosmos whose structure and vicissitudes were not purely determined by the whims of higher powers marked, in ancient Greece, the beginning of a new phase in Western culture. The idea of mathematical harmony was of far-reaching significance for music as well as medical science. The numerical, symmetric relationships in the macro and microcosm (nature and man) and the harmonious order in music as described and developed in particular by Pythagoras (5th century B.C.) and his followers offered the physician in antiquity a theoretical framework within which the use of music as a therapeutic medium could be rationalized. Pythagoras himself was thought to have made regular use of musical 'catharsis' during which the participants were carried to a 'loftier' mood, that is, a state of improved harmony and eurythmics with the help of lyre playing and singing.

As is known, the physicians of classical antiquity further developed this Pythagorean harmony for physiology and pathology into a system of harmony and disharmony of the four 'cardinal' humours (blood, phlegm, yellow bile and black bile) which had consequences not only for the somatic medicine but also for psychology and psychiatry. For instance, the terminology formed around the phenomenon of melancholy in the restricted sense was characterized by a depressive mood as the main symptom, a part of the ancient theory of humours.

Throughout the centuries, the idea of a mathematical harmony of music has been able to hold its

The disgruntled alchemist. Woodvut from the Distilling Book (Liber de arte distulandi simplicia et composita) by Hieronymus Brunswig (1509), an illustration appearing in the chapter 'The proper help and thorough cure in the treatment of Atre Bilis of the Humours and how you should conduct yourself before resorting to medication'.

ground in medical science, including the history of psychiatry. One example from the long series of ancient medical authors could be Celsus (about 25 B.C. -50) who in his *De Medicina* recommended the playing of music and the use of noise for the purpose of relieving patients with depressive complaints from their ailment. This latter advice reveals the persistent thought that mental illness is not only a disturbance (a dyscrasia) of the harmony of mind and body, but that it is also determined by the presence of demons which are intimidated not so much by the quality but rather the quantity of sound.

In medieval culture one encounters again the ancient idea of numerical harmony in music, cosmos and human body, for example in the writings of Anicius Boethius (about 480-524). According to this philosopher-physician, the connection between the macrocosm and the celestial spheres can be conceived as a 'musica mundana', whereas the human microcosm encompassed the 'musica humana'. Therefore, if the order in the human body became disturbed in relation to the established order provided by the macrocosm, then the right balance could be restored by means of 'musica instrumentalis'.

The development of religious music can also hardly be ignored, considering the use of music therapy for depressions (of course, not only religious depressions). Already in early Christian tradition, but primarily in the mystical movements of medieval Christianity, music developed into the ideal medium for elevating man from the abyss of everyday terrestrial struggle to the higher harmonious spheres of the divine. In this thinking, the Pythagorean 'musica mundana' became the music of angels to which the mystical worshippers could listen in Divine Contemplation. From this period, the music of Hildegard von Bingen (1098-1180), an abbess and mystic who also practised medicine, is the best-known and undoubtedly the most fitting example. It can be assumed that exercising such musical influence on the human affects was also of considerable significance in the treatment of depressive moods.

Hugo van der Goes

The most widely known story from medieval literature about depressions and music concerns Hugo van der Goes (1440-1482), the famous master of Flemish art. His talents as a painter found undisputed acclaim among his contemporaries. At a young age he was already commissioned to carry out a variety of great painting assignments, primarily for magnificent projects of a religious nature. His most famous painting was delivered in about 1475 to the Medici representative in Bruges: the triptych of the Portinari altarpiece, presently in Florence, with a larger than life-size depiction of the Adoration of the Shepherds.

In 1475, at the pinnacle of his fame, Van der Goes surprised friend and foe by unexpectedly entering the Red

The centre panel of the triptych of the Portinari altarpiece, painted by Hugo van der Goes (Uffizi, Florence).

Cloister (Rooklooster) of the Canons Regular in the Zoniënwoud near Brussels as a lay brother. His half-brother Nicolaas had already been a monk there for many years. The reason for this sudden turnabout was supposedly rooted in a depression, a melancholy disorder that caused him to renounce a further life in secular spheres, and which was accompanied by guilt feelings and self-condemnation, as well as thoughts of suicide. Art historians believe that the development of this depressive disorder can be recognized by the heightened restlessness emanating from his paintings. Given this art-historical characterization, one obviously thinks in terms of a manic-depressive psychosis, a syndrome which in the Middle Ages was placed under the common denominator of melancholy.

The illness, however, only manifested itself after several years (1480/1) in an unmistakable manner as a depressive psychosis, referred to by a contemporary as a 'mirabilis fantasialis morbus'. At the time, Van der Goes was in the company of a party that had visited Cologne and was making the return journey to the cloister near Brussels. The precise course of events is recorded in the convent chronicles, the *Catalogus fratrum choralium Rubeae Vallis* of Caspar Ofhuys (1456-1523) who was a novice there at the same time as Van der Goes.

Ofhuys writes: 'Brother Nikolaas told me that one night during the return journey Brother Hugo was overcome by a peculiar illness of the imaginative powers; he started to lament incessantly that he was a reprobate and sentenced to eternal damnation. He would even have taken his own life if his travelling companions had not prevented this with the use of force. As a result of Van der Goes' peculiar illness the journey came to a sad end.'

Presumed self-portrait of Hugo van der Goes (about 1440-1482), depicted in the centre panel of the Monforte altarpiece (Daglem, Berlin).

'The mentally ill brother was escorted to Brussels where he was placed under the supervision of the prior, Father Thomas. After close observation, the prior came to the conclusion that Van der Goes suffered from the same psychic disorder as King Saul. He remembered how Saul's restlessness had been alleviated by David's harp-playing and therefore gave his immediate consent to rendering music in the presence of the sick brother. In addition to musical instruments, they could also avail themselves of the vocal achievements of the convent choir and of any other means that might be able to drive away the "fantasies" of the mental patient.'

In his account, Ofhuys emphasized the reactive moment in the genesis of Van der Goes' disorder. According to him, the case of Van der Goes did not concern a 'frenesis magna' (great frenzy), since the mentally ill painter had never attempted to harm another person. There were two possibilities. The first possibility was that it involved a natural illness, a melancholy caused by eating improper food, drinking strong wine and by emotions. Furthermore, Van der Goes' worrying about painting assignments were thought to have had an adverse effect. The second possibility was that Brother Hugo's illness was a dispensation of God, intended to discourage in Van der Goes the kind of pride that would make him lose his soul.

Medieval and early modern perceptions of music therapy

The shift from the metaphysical to the physical, from the scholastic contemplation of nature to the humanist nature studies, also had consequences for the manner in which the connection between melancholy and music was perceived. In the relation between demonologic thinking and the explanation according to the ancient doctrine of the four 'cardinal humours' – two parallel views upheld in psychiatry for a long time – the accent gradually shifted in the direction of the latter way of thinking. However, this also means that numerous speculative theories were propounded in these explanations, mostly based on the aforementioned views on the connection between macro and microcosm.

Bartholomaeus Ramis de Pareia (1440?-1500?) can serve as an illustrative example of such speculative thinking. In his *Musica practica* from 1482, this Spanish author established a connection between the four major keys and the four cardinal humours: between the 'tonus protus' and phlegm, the 'tonus deuterus' and yellow bile, the 'tonus tritus' and blood, and the 'tonus tetartus' and black bile, the cause of melancholy. Since these keys and corresponding humours were again connected with certain celestial bodies – respectively the moon, Mars, Jupiter and Saturn (the planet of depressions) – it was a matter of cosmic harmony which, according to the physician Pareia,

Illustration from 'Il Filostrato' by Giovanni Boccaccio (1313-1375) which tells about a depressive knight who was cured with the help of singing and music-playing ladies.

offered a sound basis for the application of music in his therapeutic treatments.

In addition, there were the noted representatives of Renaissance psychiatry, such as the Zierikzee physician Levinus Lemnius (1505-1568) and the Gouda physician Boudewijn Ronsse (1525-1597) who in his *Epistolae medicinales* (1590) asserted that a melancholy patient should first be helped with flute-playing and only subsequently with medication. Most widely known is undoubtedly Johannes Weyer or Jan Wier (1515?-1588) who in his famous book *De praestigiis daemonum et incantationibus ac veneficijs libri sex* (1568) claimed that not all melancholia sufferers are tormented by demons, but that indeed all persons tormented by demons are also suffering from melancholy disorders.

In theological literature it was generally taken for granted that Saul's case concerned a demonic illness. However, there existed an interesting difference of opinion between the two great church reformers, John Calvin (1509-1564) and Martin Luther (1483-1546) about the role music played in the recovery process. Calvin considered the belief that music had a healing effect one of the misconceptions of 'profane human beings'. In his opinion, they ignored the fact that David's harp was only an external means, and that the alleviation of Saul's disorder was brought about by God Himself. Others, in particular medieval authors, suggest that the curative effect the music had on Saul was solely due to the cross-shaped arrangement of the strings on the musical instrument played by David. It was the allegorical form depicting the cross of Christ which caused the evil spirit in Saul to take flight.

Contrary to his kindred soul from Geneva, Luther – himself a passionate lover and practitioner of music and religious song, and also not unfamiliar with depressions – expressed the opinion in one of his so-called 'Table Talks' (1532) that the story of David and Saul was primarily intended to convince Christians of the value of music therapy. 'The devil is a sad spirit (spiritus tristiae) and makes people sad, and that is why he cannot bear cheerfulness. For this reason, he flees as far away from music as possible, and does not remain, especially when spiritual songs are sung. This is how David with his harp alleviated Saul's attacks whenever the devil tormented him.'

With this conviction, Luther recommended in a letter written in 1534 to Hieronymus Weller to immediately start making music and singing whenever sadness threatened to get the upper hand: 'Therefore, whenever thou art dejected and sadness wants to overwhelm you, then say: Come, I must play a song on the regal for my Lord Jesus Christ, either the Te Deum or Benedictus or such, because the Scripture teaches me that He enjoys listening to cheerful song and string music. And turn immediately to the piano and accompany yourself with song until the (sad) thoughts go away, as did David and Elisha. Should the devil return and instil in you a worry or sad thought, resist immediately and say: Be off, devil, I must now sing and play for my Lord Jesus Christ.'

A new voice in this discussion came in 1531 from the authoritative theologian Thomas de Vio Cajetanus (1469-1534), who had gained a reputation as Luther's opponent at the Diet of Worms. In his commentary on the Old Testament, Cajetanus described the evil spirit of Saul not as a demon, but as a 'spiritus melancholicus' and thus moved the discussion about music therapy to the sphere of humoral pathology.

> *'It is certainly not surprising that music not only curtails the movement of the melancholy spirit, but also puts it at rest completely. Because the physical disorder passes on to the mind, and pleasant sounding music refreshes the mind and calms down the agitated movements of both the spirit and the body. Just as physical suffering affects the mind, in the reverse case the state of mind has an effect on the body. The choice of words in the text [about David and Saul] confirms, ... that with this evil spirit reference is made to*

attacks of a melancholy spirit, because otherwise it would not have been said that it had yielded to the music, which was indicated as the only reason for his cure. Moreover, the sequence of the effects of the music on Saul must not be overlooked. The first consequence was an 'expansion' of the heart, precisely the opposite usually encountered in a melancholy disorder. Because in the latter case the spirit contracts; on the other hand, joy causes it to expand. This explains why Saul felt better and was ultimately delivered from his melancholy condition. Because natural remedies have a gradual effect.'

The fact that the medieval idea of the 'melancholia balneum diaboli', melancholy as the bath of the devil, has continued to exist for a long time is confirmed in the popular periodical *Philosophische Luststunden* (Philosophical Pleasure Hours). In it, the theologian and physician Christian Franz Paullini (1643-1712) described in 1706 how the story of Saul has taught that the devil had his 'Badstuben' (bathhouse) in the melancholy humours. By removing these fluids, the devil(s) would also be driven away. Such a conception of matters reveals a marvellous combination of natural and supernatural thinking with regard to the cause of depressions.

Music therapy and depression

That music therapy can boast an uninterrupted tradition on the podium of medical history has been made possible in part by repeated changes of the décor. By merely adapting the justification of music's therapeutic effect time and again to the new insights which had come to determine medical-scientific thinking, music could for centuries retain its place in the therapeutic repertory of the general practitioner. In fact, the same can be said about numerous other therapies. For instance, the use of phlebotomy, whose foundations were purely empirical, could be maintained for centuries by repeatedly adapting its legitimization to the altered circumstances at an early stage.

On the basis of several works from medical and psychiatric literature, a selection of views regarding the beneficial use of music in the treatment of psychic disorders in general, and depressive disorders in particular, is offered to illustrate this process.

In the latter part of the Middle Ages, the theologian, philosopher and physician Marsilio Ficino (1433-1499) was a well-known and confirmed supporter of music therapy in treating melancholy disorders. In his book *De vita libri tres* (1489), in which Ficino describes, among other things, the illness of scholars (see volume 4 of this series), one finds an elaborate argumentation regarding the influence which listening to music has on the melancholy state of mind. According to Ficino, music consisted of a vibration of the air, as a result of which it was

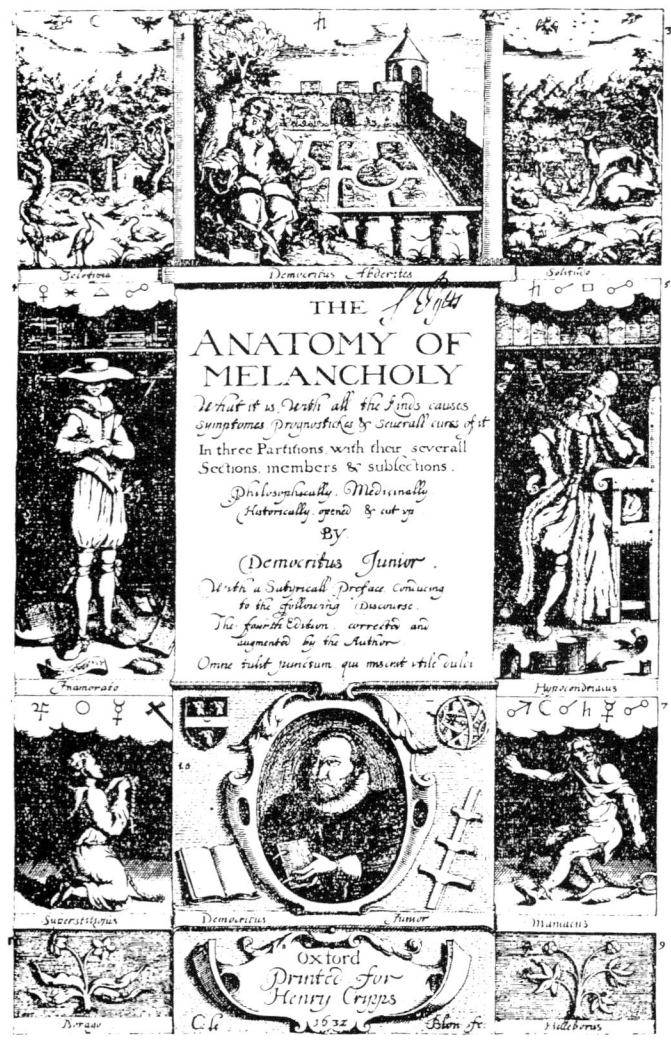

Title page of Richard Burton's 'The Anatomy of Melancholy'

in a position to exercise an elevating and refining effect on the spirit. Aside from this influence on the mental part of man, music also had a stimulating effect on the physical part. Music was therefore able to take hold of the entire human being. In this connection, Ficino also defended the interesting view that in therapy the melancholy patient must also personally play and, if possible, compose music. In this manner, music was introduced as an exogenous as well as endogenous remedy aimed at restoring the harmonious mixture (eukrasia) of the humours.

For the early 17th century, the *Anatomy of Melancholy* (1621) by Richard Burton (1576-1640) is the undisputed standard work on the category of disorders among which depressions can be rated. On the basis of dozens of examples, Burton demonstrates the value of music therapy in the treatment of melancholy illnesses: 'In a word, it is so powerful a thing that it ravisheth the soul, *regina sensuum*, the queen of the senses, by sweet pleasure (which is a happy cure), and corporal tunes pacify our corporal soul; *sine ore loquens, dominatum in animum exercet* [speaking without a mouth, it exercises domination over the soul] and carries it beyond itself, helps, elevates, extends it ... It is a sovereign remedy against de[s]pair and melancholy, and will drive aw[a]y the devil himself.' For an explanation with regard to the working mechanism of music therapy, Burton refers his readers to the scholarly humanist Josephus Justus Scaliger (1540-1609) who wrote that the spirit became a part of the vibrating and dancing air which the music channeled into the body. As a result, the spirit was put in motion and the sadness was driven away.

Iatro-musica

Despite the new mathematical-inductive direction taken by medicine at the end of the 16th century and the gradual disappearance of ancient outlooks on cosmic and physiological events, music was also held in high esteem as a therapeutic remedy in the second half of the 17th century. A special school of thought had even developed, the so-called 'iatro-musica', which claimed a central position for music in diagnostics (pulse beat and music!) and therapy. The well-known theologian and natural scientist Athanasius Kircher (1601-1680), who represented this school of thought, dedicated in his book *Musurgia universalis* (1650) an entire chapter to this 'Magia musurgico iatrica'. He captivated his contemporaries primarily with expositions on resonance and vibration phenomena.

According to Kircher, sound was able to harbour a hidden power which was in a position to influence certain processes in the human body. This was the case whenever a specifically proportioned, harmonious air movement encountered an equally proportioned (part of the) body and put it into motion by means of resonance. Once familiar with these specific measures and relationships existing between the sound of a musical instrument and the spirit, and between the muscles and veins of the human body, one could easily put human beings into any affective state desired. Once the proportional connection between music and the four humours had been established, no illness – no matter how persistent and deep-rooted – would be able to resist the power of music therapy. In his posthumously published treatise *Phonurgia nova* (1684), Kircher developed this theory even further, hereby making use of the new (Cartesian) idea that the healing effect of music was due to the influence of sound on the particles in the sensorium (the soul).

The acrid spirit and vapours in the brain of the melancholy patient are set in motion by the air vibrations caused by the music; subsequently they are heated and diluted. The black bile is dissolved and then withdraws from the brain and ultimately leaves the body as a vapour (through perspiration). On the other hand, spirit and vapours could be curbed in their movement and pacified by very slow tones and small intervals. The spirits thus withdrew from the melancholic humour and deprived it of

Athanasius Kircher (1601-1680), prominent representative of the 'iatro musica'.

its effectiveness, because they all rushed to the ear to hear the lovely music, to subsequently return quietly once again. It is interesting to observe how Kircher sketches David's course of action as that of an experienced music therapist. He was not only an excellent musician, but also recognized very precisely the affects and illness of his patient. He also knew how to adapt the music to the condition of the four humours and understood how to select the proper rhythm in order to please the patient.

Music and depression in the Age of Reason

From the examples given it clearly emerges that the ancient doctrine of the four humours, combined with the spirit as guiding principle of body and mind, continued to determine the thinking with regard to the therapeutic effect of music in the treatment of physical and psychic disorders. Only in the course of the 18th century did the so-called 'systematists', among which Herman Boerhaave (1668-1738) and Friedrich Hoffmann (1660-1742), develop medical systems in which tangible parts of the body were also assigned a place in physiology and pathology. In this so-called 'solidism', body tissues played a significant role; in neurology, nerve tissue became the most important subject of study.

Ultimately, this development also influenced the views held with regard to the effect of music therapy on neurotic and mentally ill persons. Initially, both explanations for the different elements of pathology could be found side by side; subsequently, a differentiation within one clinical picture was established for both explanatory models. Finally, in the second half of the 19th century humoral pathology definitely gave way to solidism in the form of cellular pathology.

As far as melancholy was concerned, Boerhaave, for example, was backing ancient humoral pathology, even though in his definition of melancholy the 'idée fixe' (obsession) is named as a characteristic (aphorism 1089). Among the 'natural' and 'artificial' remedies against melancholy which Boerhaave lists in his *Aphorismi*, no

Portrait of Johannes Augustus Unzer (1727-1799).

mention is made of music. However, it shall later become apparent from another source that in his treatment of melancholy patients Boerhaave did indeed assign a role, though modest, to music.

The Parisian physician Anne-Charles Lorry (1726-1783) went a step further and in his study *De melancholia et morbis melancholicis* (1765) made a distinction between two forms of melancholy: one was the result of an excess of black bile (humoral pathology), while the other could be ascribed to a disturbed functioning of the nerve tissue (solidism). The latter form became known under the name of 'mélancholie nerveuse' or 'Neuromelancholia'. In the special chapter which Lorry dedicated to music therapy, he attributed the principal effect of music to a general relaxation of the body tissue.

However, the 18th century physicians sought the most important foundations for their therapeutic regimen in an extensive hygiene, a 'regimen sanitatis', which was aimed at maintaining the equilibrium of the so-called 'sex res non-naturales', namely the air, eating and drinking, sleeping and waking, exercise and rest, excretion and secretion and, last but not least, the 'affectus animi' (state of mind). A sound regimen, and therefore also a good therapy, included an adequate diet, the use of medication and exercising an influence on the affects by means of music. This regimen has been expounded in numerous popular-scientific works.

For instance, in one of his 'spectatorial expositions' about *Der Arzt or The Physician* (which was also published in a Dutch translation), the German physician Johannes Augustus Unzer (1727-1799) gives an essay on the 'Medicinal Usefulness of Music in Many Illnesses', in which he sings the praises of music therapy in the treatment of depressions.

'In all types of mental illnesses, bewildering emotions exist, and music is able to pacify them, and in this manner can contribute to the cure of this illness. That music exercises this effect on the emotions through a natural power becomes apparent from the unquestionable example of a two-year old child, born and raised by parents who were lovers and practitioners of music; the child became

extremely cheerful when its parents played a number of light-hearted pieces and, on the other hand, fell into a state of deep melancholy as soon as it heard sad or even very serious tones – a condition that persisted until the child's adverse state was driven away again by cheerful music.'

It is remarkable that Unzer firmly rejected the use of music therapy as a panacea:

'Care should hereby be taken to ensure that these physicians themselves are authorities on music and that they are able to judge from the patient's condition which type of emotions should be aroused or pacified in them and in which way, and what type of music must be used for this purpose. Whoever attempts to cure mental patients with the use of music and neglects to make such a close distinction, would act as inconsistent as if he tried to dispel all fevers with powders.'

A delightful description of the manner in which this regimen and music in particular are administered in the case of depressions can be found in a letter written in 1739 by Boerhaave's student, Gerard van Swieten (1700-1772), to the Russian court-physician Antonio Ribēiro Sanches (1699-1783). In this letter, the Viennese physician recounts how his teacher had once given him the advice 'to pacify the more severe Muses with the sweet entrancement of music, whereby he [Boerhaave, v.L.] had assured him that he himself had derived great comfort from it when he had suffered from the same melancholy disorder'. It is known from other sources that Van Swieten closely followed Boerhaave's advice by playing music for approximately two hours every week.

This regimen, which was aimed at the cure and later the prevention of his melancholy (better known as 'scholar's hypochondria'), formed the musical environment in which his son Gottfried van Swieten (1734-1803) was raised. His name, which is closely associated with the Viennese history of music, can be found in the biographies of Haydn, Mozart and Beethoven. In their careers, all of them had regular and intensive contact with the young Van Swieten, a fact that should not be left unmentioned seeing the extent to which depressions played a role in their lives.

A new age dawned in the 18th century for music therapy in general, and for music therapy in the treatment of mental and neurological illnesses in particular. After René Descartes (1596-1650) had introduced the conceptual distinction between body and mind into medical science, and since on the basis of the so-called corpuscular thinking iatrophysics and iatrochemistry had started to flourish, various physicians from the early 18th century started to devote themselves to the characteristics and workings of the human mind, either in connection with somatic medicine or not. It was this exploration of the fringe area between body and soul, combined with numerous new insights in neurophysiology and a general reassessment of affective expressions in literature and the arts, that opened up a vast perspective for music therapy.

The publication of the well-known book by Ernst Anton Nicolai (1722-1802) from Halle (Germany) entitled *Die Verbindung der Musik mit der Artzney-Gelahrtheit* (1745) (The Connection of Music with Medical Science) was part of the overture to this new era. Nicolai was the first author who focussed not so much on the physical phenomena of musical sound but on the psychological reactions resulting from listening to music. According to him, the therapeutic effect of music was due to its affect-evoking impulse transmitted to the emotional life of the human being.

Music therapy in the Age of Enlightenment

Numerous examples can be given of the pre-18th century application of music therapy in the treatment of depressive disorders. The rich variety of musical styles, from baroque and rococo to classicism and romanticism, and the achievements of the great masters, among which Bach, Handel, Haydn, Mozart and Beethoven, make this century an indisputable high point in the history of music. For monarchs, nobility and the upper bourgeoisie, music was the ideal means for breaking the long days of monotony and solitude. They acted as patrons to a flock of musicians and composers for whom there was hardly enough work to earn their daily bread in and around the concert halls of the European cultural centres. Engaging the services of talented musicians and great composers was a matter of status and honour for them, especially when it concerned child prodigies, composers who appealed to their patron's musical taste or musicians who knew how to touch the right chords of a large audience.

At the same time, the 18th century has the reputation of being the nervous century that offered ample space in literature, the visual arts and music for expressing a troubled and shaken inner life. This certainly applies to the second half of the 18th century which saw the breakthrough of Romanticism. The leading figures from the literature of this period are widely known: one of the earliest representatives in England was Edward Young (1683-1765) with his *Night Thoughts on Life, Death and Immortality*; in Germany it was Johann Wolfgang von Goethe (1749-1832) with his book *Die Leiden des jungen Werthers* (The Sorrows of Young Werther), among others; in France, Jean Jacques Rousseau (1712-1778) and his novel *Julie ou la Nouvelle Héloise* (Julie or the New Heloise); and in the Netherlands, Rhijnvis Feith (1753-1824) with such novels as *Julia* (1783) and *Ferdinand en Constantia* (1785).

Where the interaction between depression and music is concerned, both characteristics of the 18th century would have to touch one another on several points. On the one hand, it could be expected that the depressive emotional state of musicians is expressed in their work; on the other hand, an important therapeutic role has been ascribed to music in dealing with the disturbed inner life.

A general examination of these two expectations is not within the scope of the popular-scientific review at hand. Prudence, and even a certain scepticism, seem to be in order. Establishing too close a link between depression and music could easily mean shortchanging the marvellous complexity of musical creativity and ignoring the frequently still obscure paths and detours of the psychology of music. Only an exemplary account of both musical expression and music therapy in the 18th century's history of depression can help to further illustrate the general connection between depression and music.

Carlo Broschi Farinelli

A prime example of 18th century music therapy in the treatment of depressions is the story of the Italian castrato singer Carlo Broschi Farinelli (1705-1782) and his two depressive patients at the Spanish court. The leading role in this story is played by the most famous opera singer of all times, Carlo Broschi, Neapolitan by birth and generally known under the name of Farinelli. At an early age, Farinelli was already one of the celebrated representatives of Italian opera; he had his first performance in 1722 when he sang in Porpora's opera *Eomene* in Rome. He was highly successful, not only in his own country, but also elsewhere in Europe. High points of his career were the performances in London during the years 1734-1736, where in the Lincoln's Inn Fields Theatre he reaped the admiration of English audiences for his role in the opera *Artaserse*. His singing voice, with a range of more than three octaves, effortlessly passed the high C, and with its pathos and simplicity easily enthralled the hearts of his large audiences.

Carlo Broschi Farinelli (1705-1784), opera singer and music therapist at the Spanish court.

During 1737 Farinelli's brilliant career took a most peculiar turn. Responsible for this change of course was the Spanish royal house of Bourbon, a dynasty troubled by hereditary mental illness which expressed itself in deep depressions, often culminating in early and complete insanity. This also applied to the monarchs of the House of Bourbon reigning in Farinelli's days.

After the Peace of Utrecht (1713) which brought an end to the War of the Spanish Succession, Philip V (1683-1746) – grandson of Louis XIV and Maria Teresa of Spain, the daughter of Philip IV (1605-1665) – acceded to the throne as the first Bourbon king of Spain. The prodigious melancholy of this young monarch had already manifested itself for quite some time. As a result of this disorder, he lapsed into an extraordinary inertia and depression which made him unfit for everything. 'His humour is so black that he is not touched by anything, and he has confessed to me that life itself was a burden to him,' wrote Louville, his court-physician. It is therefore not surprising that Philip left governing to his wives, Maria Luisa of Savoy and later Elizabeth Farnese of Parma.

After the death of his son, Philip's depressions reached a low point. From then on, he spent his days in bed, let his hair and nails grow, cloaked himself in deepest silence and only got up at night for a bite to eat. There was only one thing, namely a singing voice, that seemed to have an influence on the condition of the 'lypemaniac' in the Madrid palace. In 1737 his wife, Elizabeth Farnese, brought the name of Farinelli, the famous opera singer whom she still knew from his performances in Parma and Ferrara, to the attention of Philip V.

In early August 1737, Farinelli made the actual acquaintance of the mentally ill king. In a room adjacent to Philip's chambers a concert was organized in which Farinelli was to present his artful singing. He had hardly finished his first aria when the king showed himself deeply touched. After the second aria he summoned the singer to his chamber, showered him with compliments and requested a third performance. After the concert, the king – overwhelmed by so much musical beauty – asked Farinelli how he wished to be rewarded. He would not be refused anything. With his reply, Farinelli sealed his fate for the next quarter-century of his life: he asked the king to get up, groom himself, forget his depression and devote himself to government affairs. Soon after, to everyone's amazement, Philip V appeared in the Council of State.

As a result, no efforts were spared in an attempt to tie the Italian castrato singer to the court in Madrid. Showered with accolades, Farinelli received a lifetime position, a princely salary, living quarters in the royal palace as well as a country house, and he could freely make use of the royal stables and court personnel. Not a day passed anymore without Farinelli being summoned to the king's chambers around midnight, in order to dispel the monarch's depressions with his singing. He then sang his arias four hours long, accompanied by the royal orchestra, and talked with Philip V about the most diverse subjects.

From reports of contemporaries, and particularly from the study made by the Austrian music historian Franz Haböck, it is known which pieces Farinelli performed night after night, altogether about 3600 times. They were two arias from the aforementioned opera *Artaserse* by Johann Adolf Hasse, namely the *Pallido il Sole* and the *Per questo dolce amplesso*. The third piece rendered was a minuet from the opera *Fortunate passate mie pene* by Attilio Ariosti. The fourth aria was taken from the opera *Merope* by Geminiano Giacomelli and derived its beauty (and degree of difficulty!) from the imitation of a nightingale. In the course of the years, the latter piece was presented by Farinelli in a variety of renditions, as becomes apparent from Farinelli's manuscript with arias which has been preserved for posterity.

Pallido il sole.

Arie des Artabano aus der Oper „Artaserse" von Hasse.

Pallido il sole torbido il Cielo	Blaß ist die Sonne, trüb der Himmel.
Pena minaccia morte prepara	Strafe droht, Tod bereitet sich vor.
Tutto mi spira rimorso ed orror.	Alles haucht mir Reue und Schrecken zu.
Timor mi cinge di freddo gelo	Angst umklammert mich mit kaltem Frost,
Dolor mi rende la vita amara	Schmerz macht mir das Leben bitter,
Io stesso fremo contro il mio cor.	Ich selbst wüte gegen mein Herz.

Pietro Metastasio.

Per questo dolce amplesso.

Arie des Arbace aus der Oper „Artaserse" von Adolf Hasse.

Per questo dolce amplesso,	Um dieser süßen Umarmung,
Per questo estremo addio	Um dieses letzten Lebewohles willen
Serbarmi o Padre mio	Behüte mir, o Vater,
L'idolo amato.	Das geliebte Idol.
Sol questo all' ombra mia	Nur dies sei für meinen Schatten
Pace e conforto sia	Friede und Trost
Nel fier mio fato.	In meinem herben Geschick.

Pietro Metastasio.

Fortunate passate mie pene.

Arie des Arbace, Einlage zu Adolf Hasse's Oper „Artaserse" von Attilio Ariosti.

Fortunate	Sia pur d'amore	Als Glück preise ich,	Wenn bloß von Liebe stammt
Passate	Fiera l'asprezza	Was ich überstand	Die wilde Grausamkeit,
Mie pene	Breve dolcezza	An Leiden,	So wird in kurzem Zärtlichkeit
Se un bel laccio	Lo placherà.	Wenn ein schönes Band	Sie mildern.
Or in braccio	Son grate al core	Oder eine Umschlingung	Angenehm sind dem Herzen
Al mio bene	L'aspre vicende	Meiner Geliebten	Harte Schicksale,
Più costante	Quando s'arrende	Noch treuer,	Wenn schließlich unterliegt
Più amante	Crudel beltà.	Noch liebender	Grausame Schönheit.
Mi fa.		Mich macht.	

Quell' usignolo.

Arie des Epitide aus Geminiano Giacomelli's Oper „Merope",
Bearbeitung mit hinzugefügter verzierter Singstimme und Kadenzen
von Carlo Broschi Farinelli.

Quell' usignolo che innamorato	Die Nachtigall voll Liebessehnsucht
Se canta solo tra fronda e fronda	Singt einsam im dunklen Laub
Spiega del fato la crudeltà.	Und beklagt des Schicksals Grausamkeit.
S'ode pietoso nel bosco ombroso	Sie verbirgt sich scheu im schattigen Hain;
Che gli risponde con lieto core	Der ihr mit fröhlichem Herzen antwortet,
Di ramo in ramo cantando va.	Schwingt sich singend von Ast zu Ast!

Domenico Lalli.

Based on this manuscript, Haböck analyzed the virtuosity of Farinelli's singing. He described one of the variations to the fourth arias as follows: 'The vocal part written in red intended for the da capo, exceeds all previously accumulated difficulties with a truly inexhaustible surge of ever faster and faster, still longer and longer rushing runs, extremely complicated sequences of inverted mordents, trills, combinations of the Lombardian slide with trillo, note radoppiate, etc. In the closing cadence, this deluge of virtuosity rushes from a fermata once more through two octaves, from high to low, and up again in twirling trills and ends with a last mighty trill.'

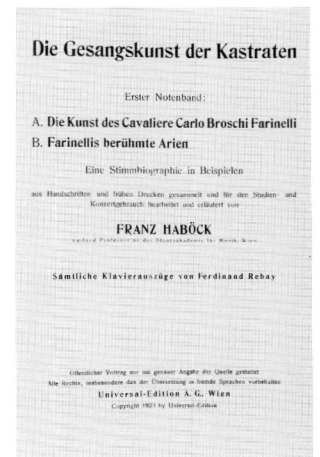

This account regarding the relationship between Farinelli and Philip V inevitably brings a comparison with the situation at the ancient Israelite court of King Saul to mind. Nevertheless, the therapeutic success was not complete, as can be concluded from the fact that the nightly sessions with the monarch tormented by melancholy continued to take place. In political life, however, Farinelli had become a vital link who could just barely manage to keep the monarch functioning at such a level that the others, in particular his wife, could handle state affairs with sufficient authority to the outside world.

Title page of 'Die Gesangkunst der Kastraten' (The Castrati's Art of Singing), Franz Haböck's study on castrato singer Carlo Broschi Farinelli.

When Philip V, the 'Einsamkeitsschwärmer' [fanatic recluse] (Haböck) died in 1746, very little changed for Farinelli. Philip's son and successor, Ferdinand VI (1713-1759) displayed the same psychic symptoms as his father. He, too, benefited a great deal from listening to the singing Italian, so that there was no question of ending Farinelli's services. However, Farinelli was given more time to devote himself to composing his own vocal music and to corresponding with the great masters of Italian opera, in particular the librettist Pietro Metastasio. Moreover, during the concerts organized at the court, he had the opportunity to make the personal acquaintance of other performing musicians.

The curtain fell for Farinelli when Ferdinand's wife, the Portuguese princess Barbara of Bragança, died in August 1758. Shortly after, the king lapsed into complete insanity. Farinelli continued to attend to the mentally ill monarch for one more year until Ferdinand's death in August 1759. He then returned to his native Italy where, in his country house near Bologna, he continued to enthrall many listeners with his voice. Farinelli, the greatest among the Italian opera singers, died in September 1782; undoubtedly the most persevering music therapist who ever ventured to undertake the treatment of a depressive patient.

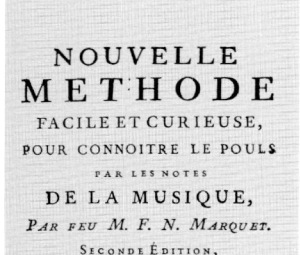

A Gallic view on melancholy

During those years, medical literature displayed a general enthusiasm for music therapy. An excellent example of this zeal is the pamphlet by François Nicolas Marquet (1687-1759) entitled *Nouvelle Méthode facile et curieuse, pour connoitre le pouls par les notes de la Musique* (Easy and unusual New Method for reading the pulse by the notes of the Music), whose second edition was published in 1769 in both Amsterdam and Paris. This version was edited by Pierre-Joseph Buchoz (1731-1807), a physician from Nancy, who also added a number of observations and critical thoughts to this booklet, as well as a 'Memoire sur la manière de guérir la mélancholie par la Musique' (Memoir on how to cure melancholy with Music).

Buchoz presented his 'Mémoir' as an interpretation of Hippocrates' 23rd aphorism: 'If fear and sadness persist for a long time, it is an indication of melancholy' (*Si metus et tristia multo tempore perseverint, melancholicum hoc ipsum*). In his interpretation of the origins of melancholy, Buchoz clearly presented himself as a follower of the aforementioned iatro-mechanician, Friedrich Hoffmann. According to him, fear and sadness cause a higher tension in the body fibres, including the fibres of the vascular walls, as a result of which the circulation of the humours stagnated and the contents of

Title page of Marquet's treatise on pulse diagnostics and music, followed by Buchoz' text on music therapy in the treatment of melancholy (1769).

the vessels thickened. He considered this thickening of the humours the direct cause of melancholy.

Buchoz further distinguished between 'mélancholie sec et humide' (dry and humid melancholy). People with a humid temperament had fibres that were feeble, which makes the oscillations of the pulse weak and the secretions sluggish. As a result, such persons are diffident, dejected and fearful. In the case of dry melancholy, the fibres are tense, the fluids thickened and the patient has a firm pulse. In addition, these latter patients have a 'wild look in their eyes, great seriousness, complete silence, they are lost in thought, have inexhaustible patience in their work, a longing for solitude, distinct preferences and aversions, gloomy predictions and sad dreams'.

According to Buchoz, it is of little use to seek help at the pharmacy, 'but one should rather resort to better, more efficient means; I am referring to music, that heavenly gift, which alleviates our sorrows and wipes away or at least diminishes the thinking of them'. No matter whether the music is vocal or instrumental, diatonic[1], chromatic[2] or enharmonic[3], it is the means by which 'sadness can be converted into joy, fear into courage, harshness into courtesy, despair into hope'.

Buchoz sought the explanation for this miraculous therapeutic effect in the transfer of sound vibrations to the fibres of the body, whereby the result of course depended on the condition of these fibres. 'Music must therefore be used for curing dry melancholic temperaments; one must start with the lowest tones and subsequently move on gradually to the higher ones. Due to the harmonic

---

1 Consisting of a natural sequence of tones, progressing by whole or half tones.
2 Scale progressing up and down by half tones.
3 Designating the use of intervals less than a half tone. The meaning of 'homophonic' only stems from the 19th century!

gradation, the rigid fibres get accustomed to the different degrees of vibration and gradually begin to slacken. On the other hand, fibres possessing a humid melancholic temperament require cheerful, vigorous, lively and varied music for their cure, since this type of music is far better suited for setting the fibres into motion and strengthening them.'

Depression and musical genius

The rich musical culture of the 18th century offers an outstanding opportunity for examining whether or not depressions are 'audibly' represented in its works. As already indicated, important hereby is the repeatedly arising, both unavoidable and relevant question regarding the relationship between depressive nature and creativity, between being a patient and being an artist, or the manner in which one should attempt to approach the psychology of the music and of the musician.

As for the alleged role which depressions are to have played in the life and work of individual musicians, it cannot be denied that many biographers have recorded the lives of the musicians admired by them in accordance with their own stereotype of the music and their own aesthetic views. In doing so, many of them pursued the idea of a special connection between genius or erudition and melancholy, as expressed, for example, in Albrecht Dürer's famous engraving *Melancolia*.

In her *Handbuch der Musikpsychologie* (1985) (Manual on Music Psychology), Helga de la Motte-Haber made the necessary critical comment on the question of the connection between genius and creativity on the one hand, and melancholy or depression on the other hand. She pointed out how famous musicians, particularly in their correspondence, frequently complained about a corporal inability and physical discomfort, almost always connected with depressive feelings, but that this did not indicate that it concerned an actual disorder. Frédéric Chopin (1810-

1849), for example, supposedly talked himself into the ailments and depressions from which he suffered by way of a self-fulfilling prophecy, whereas Robert Schumann (1810-1856) whose complex clinical history consisted to a large degree of depressive disorders, rather used this form of self-pity to free himself from his depressions. Referring to Schopenhauer's metaphor of Mont Blanc, whose top is usually shrouded in clouds, she spoke in this connection of 'a hypothesis which continues to be worth considering, [namely] to what extent the experience of sorrow, which does not have to be clearly articulated, is counterbalanced by creative production'. Furthermore, artists usually find in their artistic achievements an outlet or compensation for the psychological problems with which they are confronted. The fact that the content of these musical achievements does not need to show any relationship with the musician's existing depressive disorders has been demonstrated, among others, by the Dutch musician and medical psychotherapist Hans Henkemans.

This question could be further examined on the basis of a large number of pathographical studies. Many composers and musicians with depressions could be considered as subjects of such research. In their book *Genie, Irrsinn und Ruhm* (Genius, Madness and Fame), Wilhelm Lange-Eichbaum and Wolfram Kurth list a dozen representatives in the field of music who have suffered from depressions. It is reported that the not so widely known German composer Christian Schubart (1739-1791) was incited to musical achievement by his depressive-hypochondriac disorder; Gaetano Donizetti (1797-1848), known in psychiatric history for the introduction of the 'Wahnsinnsszene' (Mad Scene) in his opera *Lucia di Lammermoor*, was reputed to have been tormented by headaches and depressions; among the mood aberrations suffered by the aforementioned Robert Schumann, both authors ascribe an important place to depressions; in the case of Franz Liszt (1811-1886), mention is made of the months-long depression he experienced at the age of twenty; Richard Wagner (1813-1883) is diagnosed as having suffered from melancholy and a manic-depressive psychosis, in addition to several other psychiatric syndromes; Johannes Brahms (1833-1897) is described as 'trotziger Melancholiker' (obstinate melancholiac); Peter Ilich Tchaikovsky (1840-1893) suffered all his life from severe depressions; in Max Reger's (1873-1916) complex pathology, depressive disorders are also abundantly represented.

In this review it was opted for a closer examination of the life and musical work of two indisputably prominent 18th century composers, namely Wolfgang Amadeus Mozart (1756-1791) and Ludwig van Beethoven (1770-1827). Subsequently, attention will also be focussed on several representatives of the 19th and 20th century, namely Gioacchino Antonio Rossini (1792-1868), Giacomo Puccini (1858-1924) and the earlier mentioned composers, Schumann and Tchaikovsky. All of these musical virtuosi have been the subject of very comprehensive studies in which their lives and works have been analyzed in depth. They also form the subject of thorough pathographical studies which describe, sometimes in meticulous detail, the physical and psychological disorders with which these great masters had to cope.

Wolfgang Amadeus Mozart

Mozart's life was significantly marked by his youth, during which he was exploited as a child prodigy by an overly ambitious father. At the age of six, young Mozart was paraded before the European royal courts, with all the physical exertion and psychological pressure entailed in travelling. How Wolfgang experienced this demonstration of his talents has been aptly expressed in a letter written by his father, Leopold Mozart (1719-1787), on February 16, 1778: 'As a child and young man you were more serious than childlike, and when you sat at the clavier or were otherwise engaged in music, nobody dared to make even the slightest joke in your presence. Yes, your facial expression was so serious that many competent persons from different countries, at the sight of your blossoming talent and your always serious and pensive little face, seriously doubted whether you would have a long life'.

Young Mozart, the musical child prodigy.

The result of such a youth, spent in total dependence on a domineering father, was an obsessed and immature personality. Mozart's financial difficulties in his later years of life, caused in part by the life-style of his wife, Constanze Weber, only increased the burden on Mozart's psyche. In addition, he was distressed about his physical appearance which was more inclined to shock rather than please the aesthetic feeling of those around him. Mozart's small stature and large nose, the face deformed by pockmarks and the misshapen ears were constant targets of caricatural ridicule. His biographer, Johann Nepomuk Hummel, in his 'Entwurf zu einer Mozart-Biographie' (Outline of a Mozart Biography) from about 1825, added yet a psychological trait: 'He was small of stature, with a somewhat pale complexion; his physiognomy was in many ways pleasing and friendly, with simultaneously a touch of melancholic seriousness'.

A series of physical ailments ended in his mysterious death in November 1791, according to literature caused by poisoning, tuberculosis, typhus fever, septicemia, uremic coma and haemorrhagic shock (as a result of a heroic bloodletting therapy), but in all probability ascribable to an anaphylactoid purpura (Henoch-Schönlein disease), with cerebral haemorrhage and bronchopneumonia as immediate causes of death.

In the summer of 1788, after the successes of *Le nozze di Figaro* (KV 492) [1] and the opera *Don Giovanni* (KV 504), Mozart was tormented by what he himself described in a letter to his friend, the wealthy merchant and fellow-Freemason Michael Puchberg, as 'such black thoughts which I can only drive away with force'. In the same period, Mozart nevertheless succeeded in composing a clavier trio, a symphony, the 'Kleiner Marsch', a clavier sonata and an Adagio (KV 542-546), all in only ten days! The physician Reichsman, who in 1981 made Mozart the subject of his presidential address to the *American Psychosomatic Society*, rightfully referred to the difficulty of hearing the echo of his depressions in all of these works of Mozart. Who could possibly suspect a composer tormented by depressions behind Mozart's sparkling piano concerts and comic operas? According to Reichsman, there was only one exception: Mozart's last piano concert in B flat (KV 595) which was completed eleven months prior to his death. 'A mood of resignation prevails, and every stirring of energy is rejected or suppressed; and this fact makes all the more uncanny the depths of sadness that are touched in the shadings and modulations of the harmony.'

One year later, in 1789, while his wife lay seriously ill, his depressions manifested themselves with heightened intensity. For the time being, this did not interfere with Mozart's astoundingly prolific musical production. Only in the course of 1790, the influence of his disturbed psyche on his production became noticeable, at least as far as quantity was concerned. Whereas the number of compositions in the last ten years of his life (1781-1791) amounted to an average of 27 per year, his production in 1790 fell to less than one half. The following year, the year of his death, he compensated for this by publishing 34 new pieces of music.

---

1 The numbers given here are in accordance with the well-known Köchel Catalogue.

Mozart's correspondence from 1790 reveals various particulars about his depressive feelings. Especially in the exchange of letters with Puchberg, who occasionally offered the musician financial assistance, Mozart bared his emotional life. In late September 1790 he confided to Puchberg: 'If people could look into my heart, I would almost have to be ashamed. Everything inside of me is so cold, ice-cold'. And in July 1791 he wrote to his wife: 'I cannot explain my feelings to you; there is a certain emptiness which is causing me pain, a certain longing that is never satisfied, and therefore never ceases, yes, increases from day to day... I also get no joy out of my work, ... if I sit down at the clavier and sing something from the opera, I have to stop at once, it affects me too much.'

During this time (the summer of 1791), in the midst of domestic worries about his sick and pregnant Constanze who was staying at the spa in Baden near Vienna, and weighed down by depressions that made it nearly impossible for him to work, Mozart wrote his famous opera *Die Zauberflöte* (KV 620), a fantastic piece of amusement, composed to the lyrics of his masonic friend, Emanuel Schikaneder (1751-?). One month before his death, Mozart completed his splendid and joyful 'Eine kleine Freimaurer-Kantate' (KV 623), written by Schikaneder for the ceremony held on the occasion of the inauguration of the new Freemason's temple in November 1791.

His last work, which however remained uncompleted, was the famous *Requiem* (KV 626), written at the request of a mysterious visitor and commissioned by an anonymous patron (Count Walsegg-Stuppach). From a letter written during September 1791 in Italian, probably addressed to Da Ponte, with whom he was discussing the possibility of still travelling to London, we know in what kind of state Mozart was when he composed this work. 'I would like to follow your advice; but how must I do this? My head is confused. Only with great difficulty did I collect my thoughts, and the picture of this stranger [who came to request the Requiem, v.L.] won't disappear. I always see him before me, he begs, he insists, impatiently he demands the work from me. I carry on with it, because composing tires me less than resting. After all, there is nothing more for me to fear. I feel it, my condition tells me, my hour has come. I will have to die.' Mozart, one of the most celebrated creative artists in the history of music, passed away on December 5, 1791.

Ludwig van Beethoven

Ludwig van Beethoven undoubtedly enjoys the honour of being the most discussed composer in the category of pathographical literature. Ever since Alexander Wheelock Thayer wrote his famous biography about Beethoven, in which he deals at length with Beethoven's deafness, his alcohol consumption and accompanying cirrhosis of the liver, his cardiovascular complaints and a probable luetic process, it is actually no longer possible to assess him other than within the context of his physical and psychic ailments.

Miniature portrait of the young Beethoven (about 1797).

Unlike his psychic disorders, Beethoven's somatic illnesses can be easily detected in his musical work. For example, the buzzing in his ears resulting from the tympano-labyrinthic sclerosis, a process that gradually destroyed Beethoven's hearing, is thought to be recognizable in various pieces of music by a striking contrast between high descant passages and deeply rolling basses. In the cavatina of *Quartet B Flat Major* (Opus 130), Beethoven supposedly expressed the pain suffered as a result of his angina pectoris, whereas his early developed myopia is musically portrayed in the 'Duett mit zwei obligaten Augengläsern' (Duet with two indispensable eyeglasses) for violin and cello.

Observations made with regard to Beethoven's psyche primarily concern the influence of his hearing impairment on his character which increasingly more clearly displayed negative traits, mainly due to his paranoia and irritability. Beethoven's conduct was noticeably anti-authoritarian, sometimes even antisocial; Reichsman writes about him that 'he was considered insane or nearly insane'. Moreover, in their psychoanalytical study *Beethoven and his nephew* (1954), Editha and Richard Sterba draw attention to Beethoven's maternal attitude toward his brothers and the latent homosexual inclinations in this relationship. The latter was to have applied in particular to Beethoven's relationship with Karl van Beethoven, the little son of his brother Johann. The depressive mood after the break between him and Karl (1827) was expressed by Beethoven in his sad sounding 'Lento assai, cantate e tranquillo' movement of the string quartet Opus 135.

One can already read about his melancholy and depressions in Beethoven's oldest preserved letter, written shortly after his return to Vienna (1787) to Josef van Schaden. 'As long as I have been here, I have enjoyed very few pleasant hours; I am tormented the entire time by shortness of breath, and I must fear that it might develop into a consumption of the lungs; in addition to this, there is a melancholy which is nearly as much of a calamity as my illness itself.' At that time, Beethoven was not yet 17 years old!

Gradually the depressive symptoms were to become more serious, especially under the influence of his increasing deafness. In the correspondence dating from this time, one can find numerous traces of the despair with which Beethoven struggled as a result of the loss of what he himself called 'der edelste Teil' (the most noble part). The climax of this despair is documented in the so-called *Heiligenstadt Testament*, a composition written in October

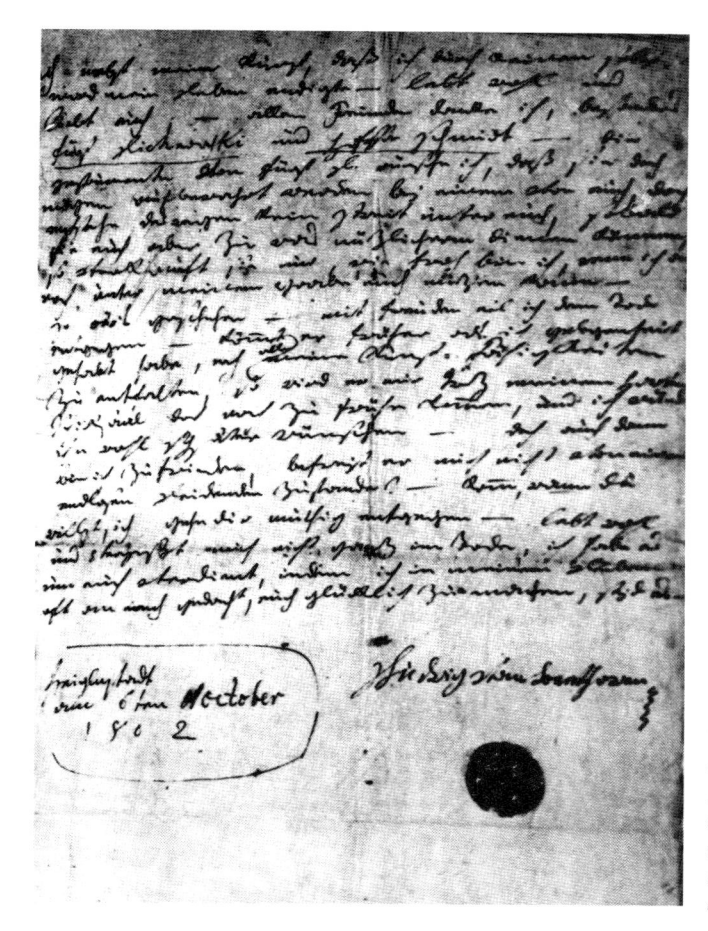

The so-called 'Heiliger-Städter Testament', written by Ludwig van Beethoven in 1802, in which he describes his despair resulting from his increasing deafness.

1802 and intended for his two brothers. 'Bear in mind, that a disastrous state has overwhelmed me since six years. ... Born with a fiery and cheerful temperament, even susceptible to the distractions of society, I soon had to withdraw, spend my life in loneliness. Even though sometimes I wanted to disregard everything, oh how harshly I was then driven back by the doubly painful experiences of my poor hearing.'

Oil painting of Ludwig van Beethoven (1770-1827), made in 1823 by F.G. Waldmüller (Beethoven House, Bonn).

Among Beethoven's oeuvre, two works ought to be singled out in connection with his history of depressive disorders, without intending to indicate a direct link between musical achievement and psychological case history. The first work is a part of the piano sonata Opus 10 (No. 3), written in 1798. In a letter from 1823 to his biographer Anton Schindler (1798-1864), Beethoven himself points out that this work expresses the feelings of a melancholiac. He goes on to say that this composition had not been given a name because he assumed that everyone possessed sufficient 'poetic feeling' to understand the piece.

'In that time,' according to Schindler, 'everyone recognized in the largo movement of the third sonata in D, Opus 10, the psychological state of a melancholiac, with all the different nuances of light and shadow in the picture of melancholy and its phases, without the need to reveal this through a title.'

A second interpretation of the psychiatric clinical picture with which Beethoven must have been well acquainted can be found in the last movement of the string quartet Opus 18 (No. 6), brought out in 1801 by the Viennese publisher T. Mollo. There is no doubt here either that the contents make a reference to melancholy, since Beethoven himself provided this piece with the title 'La Malinconia'. However, that this did not concern a depressive disorder but rather a manic-depressive psychosis has been clearly expounded by Anne Caldwell on the basis of the musical content of this actually very short piece, with a playing time of only eight minutes and twenty seconds. According to Caldwell, Beethoven also let the theme of La Malinconia resound in the last part of the piano sonata Opus 110, 'especially in its structure, with an abundance of directional phrases and dynamic marks, but no title'.

When Beethoven wrote his La Malinconia, the manic-depressive psychosis was in fact not yet known as a combined unit. Mania was generally considered to be the consequence and final stage of depression. Only in 1851, Jean-Pierre Falret (1795-1870) raised the question of 'circular' forms of mental illnesses in his classic contribution to the *Gazette des Hospitaux*, after which Jules-Gabriel François Baillarger (1809-1890) contended in 1854 that mania and depression must be viewed as two phases of the same illness ('Folie à double forme') [Madness in dual form]. The ultimate concept of the manic-depressive psychosis was provided in 1883 by Emil Kraepelin (1856-1926).

Musical analysis of 'La Malinconia'

La Malinconia consists of 6 alternating slow and fast sections. It begins with a slow section (A: bars 1-44) that opens with a 4-bar theme. The first time, it is played by the high strings, 2 violins and viola, and sounds rather eerie (bars 1-4). The second time, it is set one octave lower and is played by the second violin, viola and cello, and sounds somewhat gloomy (bars 5-8). The third time, a diminished seventh chord adds emotion (bar 9), a *crescendo* ends in a *pianissimo* (bar 12), and is here enhanced by a dramatic shift from F to F sharp in the first violin (bars 11-12).

The 4-bar theme, even when modulated, remains static, as if inhibited, without expansion or elaboration. The theme recurs in the other slow sections (C and E). And each time, the final chord of the theme begins with an inverted turn played *on* the beat (bars 4, 8, 12, 20, 198, 202, 211). This turn gives the final chord the appearance of 'arriving slowly' – as if it were cumbersome or would require great effort to reach.

The thrice repeated theme is followed by 4 diminished seventh chords, alternating *forte* and *piano*, in a keyless painful progression (bars 13-16). Each chord begins with an inverted turn that marks the rising scale, and because of these turns, the chords appear to slowly roll into one another, as if modulating from one to the other would require great effort. The entire passage (bars 13-16) gives the impression of mental pain, enhanced by the turns, and ending in despair. The theme reappears (bars 17-20).

A fugue-like section follows at bar 21, remains *pianissimo* until bar 25 and leads into another progression of alternating *forte* and *piano* chords with inverted turns in the violins and regular turns in the viola and cello. The chords rise chromatically and twice as fast (bars 30-32) as previously (bars 13-16).

IV

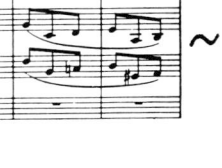

La Malinconia. ♩=58
Questo pezzo si deve trattare colla più gran delicatezza

A — Adagio

B — Allegretto quasi Allegro. ♩=88

191
C- Tempo I.
200
D- Allegretto
209
E- Adagio
F- Allegretto
217
cresc.
decresc.
270
poco Adagio
Prestissimo ♩. = 112
289
290

	Bars		Playing Time	
	from-to	total	depressed	elated
Section A	1- 44	44	3′55″	—
Section B	44-194	150	—	1′55″
Section C	195-204	10	0′55″	—
Section D	204-209	5	—	0′5″
Section E	210-211	2	0′10″	—
Section F	211-296	85	—	1′20″

Bars and playing time of 'La Malinconia', according to Caldwell 1972.

The mood begins to change in a passage of chromatically rising notes played by the cello (bars 37-42). Each note begins with an inverted turn; and the other instruments enter on the second beat with a chord. The passage begins *pianissimo* (bar 37) and ends *fortissimo* with the highest note of the entire section, the first violin's G flat (bar 42) followed by a sudden *piano* (bar 43). Then, with a half cadence, the *piano* drops to *pianissimo* (bar 44). Within that same bar, and without a break, begins the *Allegretto quasi Allegro* (section B).

This section bristles with energy and off-beat *szforzandos* add an element of restlessness (bars 45, 46 and recurring frequently throughout). Here and there are violent leaps, trill-like figures and short ascending scales until suddenly (bar 193) the cello cascades from D flat to E, crashlanding, as it were, on a desolate rock; the high strings resume their eerie chant – *pianissimo* – the *Adagio* theme (letter C), and then its gloomy repetition. But this time, on the second bar (200), the first violin enters one decime above any else, with F, so that the two violins converge as if in mental agony (bars 200-201). At letter D, the *Allegretto* now in A minor intrudes; but despite the hectic touches of the off-beat *sforzandos*, the memory of section C lingers on throughout section D. Inevitably the *Adagio* theme reappears (at letter E) for two bars, sad and final.

At letter F the *Allegretto* resumes, now in G major, a third lower than the first but every bit as tumultuous and frantic, with the familiar off-beat sforzandos. Cello and first violin jostle broken triads (bars 236-241) and a brief phrase, the first 4 notes from the *Allegretto* motif, is tossed about between all four instruments (bars 260-270). Then, after a few slow *pianissimo* bars, a very fast tempo, *prestissimo*, starts at bar 275. A *crescendo* begins at bar 280. This gets louder and louder until La Malinconia ends furiously fast, frenetic and *fortissimo*.

Depression and music in the 19th and 20th century

In the meantime, the development of psychiatry had gained momentum, particularly under the influence of enlightened thinking. The representatives of this school of thought contended that melancholy was not only linked to an intellectual nucleus ('idée fixe'), but that it also was rooted in deeper layers of the affective life. In their eyes, music was the pre-eminently suited medium for reaching these deeper layers. After all, it reaches the affective regions without having passed the filter of rational conceptions.

It would lead too far to introduce at length the most important representatives of this new school of thought, each in the context of the corresponding national developments in psychiatry and music, prior to citing their opinions with regard to the role of music therapy. Let us therefore come to the point straightaway and present the most important spokesmen.

Johann Christian Reil (1759-1813), on occasion also referred to as the German Pinel, was the foremost representative of psychiatry in Germany. In his book *Rhapsodieen über die Anwendung der psychischen Curmethode auf Geisteszerrüttungen* (Rhapsodies on the application of the psychic Method of Cure in mental derangements), published in Halle in 1803, he argues in favour of the application of the so-called 'psychic cure', which also included music among its repertory. According to Reil, the use of music was the oldest and best-suited

Title page of Rhapsodies... psychic Method of Cure (1803) by J.C. Reil

Portrait of Johann Christian Reil (1759-1813).

means for exercising a direct influence on the psyche. 'By means of inarticulated tones, music speaks to our ear and through it immediately to our heart, without first – as in rhetoric – making its way through the imagination and the mind. Music appeals to our feelings, arouses our emotions and gently entices them to surface from the depths of our soul. Music soothes the turmoils of the soul, lifts the fog of depression and sometimes restrains the unruly tumult of insanity with the best results. That's why music is often beneficial in treating insanity, and almost always in the case of the mental derangement that accompanies depression.' Reil meticulously differentiated between the various forms of illness where the use of music was advisable, and pointed out the need to carefully select both the type of music and the musical instruments.

Reil's English colleague, Joseph Mason Cox (1762-1822) also believed that, based on the same considerations, he had to give ample space to music in his therapy, which included moral treatment as well as occupational therapy. In his *Practical Observations on Insanity* (London 1804), he talks about having seen patients who had plunged into a deep lethargy and only with the help of music had regained their self-confidence. As an example, Cox presented the case of a soldier who had become insane and who had not left his bed for weeks, had not spoken a single word and had only accepted nourishment when he was forced to do so. At a certain point in time, the idea was conceived to let a minstrel come to his bedside. Cox writes: 'He played the most varied melodies and alternated them according to the effect they appeared to produce. At first his performance stimulated the patient's attention, subsequently the music aroused his interest, as was clearly visible from his suddenly lively eyes and the cheerful manner in which he kept time with the music... The beat of the music brought back memories to him [the soldier] which left behind a lively impression, aroused new thoughts and, in fact, gradually seemed to disperse the aberrations of his mind. And with the help of only this means, the patient soon got up again, dressed himself, and ultimately regained his full mental health without making it necessary to resort to other medicines (aside from light tonics).'

If we turn our ear to the representatives of French psychiatry around 1800, we can hear the same sounds about the role of music in psychiatry and in the treatment of depressive patients. For example, the philosopher and sensualist Pierre-Jean Georges Cabanis (1757-1808) wrote in his *Rapports (Traité) du Physique et du Moral de l'Homme* (1802) (Reports [Treatise] on the Physique and Morale of Man) about the ability of music to exercise in the body an immediate effect on the inner life. 'There are special sound associations and even very simple tones which simultaneously take possession of all sensory powers and via an immediate effect, directly evoke certain feelings in the soul... Hypersensitivity, melancholy, dull pain, exaggerated cheerfulness, joy bordering on madness, belligerent fervour, rage can be quickly aroused and quickly soothed with remarkably simple songs. The more unaffected these songs and the more easily comprehensible the lyrics, the more certain this effect is to occur. All these impressions apparently belong to the realm of feelings, and the brain acts hereby only as the centre of sensitivity.'

The scepticism of French psychiatry

However, the wave of enthusiasm for music therapy in psychiatry did not last very long. Especially in French psychiatry, interest faded quite rapidly. Pinel's disciple, Jean-Etienne-Dominique Esquirol (1772-1840), provides us with the best example of this in the (short) analysis of music therapy in his book *Des maladies mentales* (Paris 1838) [On Mental Illnesses]. He writes: 'I have often used music, but only very rarely did I obtain a

Jean-Etienne-Dominique Esquirol (1772-1840), the foremost disciple of Pinel and a sceptic with regard to the value of music therapy in the treatment of mental illness.

favourable result with this medium. It pacifies the mind, but it does not cure. I saw mentally ill patients who became violent as a result of the music; the one, because he thought all tones were off-key, the other, because he considered it dreadful that they were amusing themselves in the presence of an unhappy man such as he.' According to Esquirol, the authors of classic medicine had overestimated the curative effect of music, 'as so many other things'.

Critical and sceptical as he was, Esquirol believed that literature offered insufficient factual information to allow a definitive opinion on the value of music therapy and the circumstances under which it could be useful. Nevertheless, music certainly remained an excellent means particularly for convalescents, and therefore should not be ignored, 'no matter how vague the principles of its application, nor how uncertain its effect may be'.

Esquirol himself believed that success could only be achieved with music if a limited number of instruments were selected, if the musicians were positioned out of the patient's view and if the patients were subjected to pieces of music known to them from their youth or which prior to the illness had been experienced as pleasant. As an example of a less fortunate result of music therapy, Esquirol introduced his readers to a melancholy patient who was a passionate music lover. When she was being treated by Esquirol at the Salpêtrière Clinic, she repeatedly started to play and sing, 'but after only a few moments the singing stopped and she began to strike continuously several keys of the piano, and this in the most monotonous and wearisome manner for several consecutive hours, unless an effort was made to distract her and remove her from the instrument'.

In the summers of 1824 and 1825, Esquirol organized in his clinic of Salpêtrière a large-scale, interest awakening experiment, in which he wanted to examine the effects of music on a group of psychiatric patients. 'Eighty mentally ill women, which he had selected from convalescent, manic, mildly monomaniac and several melancholy patients, were acommodated in the convalescents' dormitory, next to a room in which musicians had taken up position. They played and sang melodies in a variety of tonalities and tempi, changing the number and type of instruments used. The patients were very attentive, their faces brightened up, the eyes of some of the patients became clearer, but they remained calm; some had tears streaming down their faces.' Nevertheless, Esquirol felt compelled to draw the conclusion that this musical group experiment, even though it had not been entirely without effect, could not be considered a success, in the sense that it had not resulted in the cure of a single patient, not even an improvement of their condition. 'I do not conclude from these failed experiments, 'Esquirol added, 'that it is completely useless to offer music to the mentally ill or perhaps even prompt them to play music themselves; because even if music does not cure, it at least provides distraction and in this manner alleviates the ailment.' Convalescents in particular benefited from music therapy, which is reason enough not to disregard it.

In addition to Esquirol's line of reasoning, this period of French psychiatry also offers the interesting account of Esquirol's disciple, François Leuret (1797-1851). In his book *Du traitement moral de la folie* (1840) (On the moral treatment of madness), Leuret tells about the cure of a depressive musician whom – during treatment – he let choose between a horrible douche and playing the violin. After some hesitation, the patient took the violin and played the Marseillaise! '...While he played, I led him to a school; they were singing there, and he accompanied the singers on his instrument. A full hour elapsed, during which he never stopped playing. He went on playing the following days, even though not in the best of moods. From time to time, I felt compelled to remind him that there was a douche in the proximity of the school, but I did not have to use it.

Gradually his facial expression improved and his playing, which initially had been dreadfully slow, became livelier.'

Once the patient had recovered from his illness, Leuret asked himself critically if this result was owed exclusively to the music. 'Has the music exercised the kind of influence on this patient ascribed to it by the ancient writers? Or has P. only recovered because by playing music he had taken up his old profession again? In my opinion, both factors have contributed to this recovery, and I don't know which one of the two should be considered principally responsible for the result.'

Soon after, this scepticism of French psychiatry via-à-vis the therapeutic benefit of music was to become standard practice in the treatment of mental patients. In the no-restraint system, and under the banner of occupational therapy, the high expectations held for music therapy returned to more realistic proportions and, as mentioned before, music became an element of the general care of the psychiatric patient. The scientific scepticism of the first half of the 19th century, which frequently turned into a (therapeutic) nihilism, and subsequently the thinking in terms of natural sciences which dominated medicine (and psychiatry) in the second half of the 19th century, hardly left any more room for the difficultly explained effect of music on the human body and the human mind. In any case, the neurophysiological and biological-psychiatric interpretation of psychiatric clinical pictures fell short of explaining something about the influence of music on the human psyche, healthy or sick. If attempts were made at all to link music therapy to modern, natural-science-oriented physiology and pathology, the arguments sounded rather unconvincing.

A nice example is the theory of the otherwise unknown physician Schneider who in 1835 published a treatise in which he ascribed characteristic psychological effects to the various instruments of an orchestra. In an analogous manner, much like the localization theory had been developed in neurology, Schneider wanted to show a direct connection between the musical stimulus and the psychic function. For that matter, S.E. Henschen still published a study in 1926 in which he claimed to be able to prove that each instrument in a symphony orchestra had a corresponding own (perceptive) little area in the cerebral cortex.

A depressive quartet from 19th century music

Of the four composers introduced in this chapter, Gioachino Antonio Rossini (1792-1868) is the least distinct and least complicated example. Only few people are aware of the fact that concealed behind the heavy-set figure of this great master of the *opera buffa*, known for example for his famous operas *Barber of Seville* (1816) and *William Tell* (1829), was a full-blown melancholiac. Most of his biographers agree that Rossini's depressions were related to exogenous factors, primarily his chronic gonorrhoea, a disorder complicated by urethritis and hemorrhoids. The most detailed information about his ailments can be found in the so-called Bolognese Physician's Report, a personal case history compiled in 1838 by his attending physician.

The report in question was written on the occasion of Rossini's departure to Paris where he started a new stage of life, characterized by a striking and abrupt decline in his musical production and an obsessive attention to his physical and mental state. The question is, however, if these complaints about his depression and melancholy were not intended to distract attention from his physical ailments which were considered to be rather embarrassing. Rossini appeared to symbolically conclude this stage of his life in 1864 with the composition of the *Petite Messe solennelle*, a piece that for months stirred up the emotions of music-

Photograph of Gioachino Antonio Rossini (1792-1868). taken about 1860 by N. Blanc.

loving audiences in European countries and enjoyed dozens of performances in a short period of time. It is hardly possible to imagine a more extraordinary way to mark the end of a stage of life dominated by depressions!

Of the four composers grouped together here under the common denominator of depression, Robert Schumann (1810-1856) is undoubtedly the most extreme example. The life of this musician, whose poetry also earned him a place in literary history, can be traced in detail from his extensive correspondence, his books of accounts and diaries. In these documents we become acquainted with Schumann as a man, tormented since his childhood by 'Nervenübeln' (nervous troubles). In addition, he suffered for years from an inflammation of the tendon sheath (tendovaginitis stenosans) of his right hand which ultimately made it impossible for him to play music. His pathography, however, is dominated by his melancholy, his manic-depressive psychosis and all kinds of phobias.

This is clearly reflected in the letters. In early August 1838, Schumann confided to his bride, Clara Wieck (1819-?), that all day long he had been so terribly sad, sick and deeply affected, 'that I thought my end would be near'. A few months later he reported that he frequently felt quite well, 'but even more frequently melancholy enough to shoot myself'. Here too it is striking to see how musical creativity seems to be able to manifest itself, independent of all depressions. The long series of compositions, among which his famous piano works, symphonies, operas (*Genoveva*) and, of course, the vocal music (*Liederkreis*) prove this beyond a doubt. As Schumann's pieces of music had their première, one after the other, he noted down in his diaries with the same regularity his depressive psychic feelings, his 'poor state of health', 'dizzy spells', 'great nervous debility' and 'wretched melancholy condition'.

By 1854 the psychic state of the poet-composer had worsened to such an extent, that it was necessary for him to enter a 'Nervenheilanstalt' (psychiatric clinic) near Bonn. More than two years later, Schumann died there in a state of complete insanity. The attending physician recorded in the medical report that his patient has succumbed to melancholy. 'It was the melancholy that ultimately hastened the end of the esteemed master. Whereas normally in an intensification of this illness the vegetative powers of the organism, regardless of the rapid decline of all higher powers, only seem to be little affected, it was here a question of a reversed process in so far as the mental capacities and the herewith accompanied urges,

Portrait of Robert Schumann (1810-1856).

'Nervenheilanstalt' near Bonn.

inclinations and habits could maintain themselves until the late stages of life on a relatively high, even though gradually decreasing level. On the other hand, under the influence of the heavy burden which the melancholy exercised on the nervous system, the general food intake of the body could only be upheld artificially and with great difficulty for a certain period of time. Subsequently, as a result of more frequently occurring refusals of food, an irreversible decline set in, so that due to utter emaciation, death had to follow.'

The life pattern of the Russian composer Peter Ilich Tchaikovsky (1840-1893) was entirely different, even though equally marked by melancholy. As a young man he already suffered from various psychic disorders which made his life difficult; at the age of 27 he wrote his sister that he was 'already weary of life'. To his brother he confessed in 1869: 'As a result of serious nervous disorders, I have become a hypochondriac. I really don't know why, but I feel tormented by indescribable melancholic yearnings. I would like to go away somewhere and hide in an unreachable place which has been abandoned by God.'

In his struggle against melancholy, which constantly threatened to overwhelm him, Tchaikovsky expressed his musical creativity with the production of his great compositions, such as the overture-fantasia *Romeo and Juliet*, *The Tempest*, parts of his magnificent oeuvre consisting of ten operas, six symphonies, several ballets (among which *Swan Lake* and *Nutcracker*), many piano works, cantatas, etc. Viewed against the background of his own psychic problems, his *Sérénade mélancolique* (Opus 26) for violin and orchestra, composed in 1875, deserves special mention. A year later, Tchaikovsky came in contact with Nadezhda Filaretowna von Meck (1831-1894) who became his Maecenas. From the intensive correspondence (more than 1200 letters), exchanged during the fifteen years they had been in contact with one another, one can closely follow Tchaikovsky's further development, both as a musician and a melancholiac. He remained an exceptional man in every way, even in his death, which appeared to have been the result of knowingly drinking unboiled water from the Neva River, at a time when cholera was rampant in St. Petersburg. The musical genius of the Russian history of music died a few days later of this disease.

Portrait of Tchaikovsky in 1875.

The fourth member of the quartet is the Italian composer Giacomo Puccini (1858-1924). At a young age, Puccini was already considered one of the celebrated composers of Italian opera. An early high point in his career was the performance of his opera *La Bohème* in 1896. In the period that followed, Puccini had to struggle more and more severely with his melancholy mood which developed into a depressive neurosis, accompanied by the agonizing fear of no longer being able to cope with his work. Despite everything, he nevertheless managed to compose his famous opera *Madame Butterfly*, later still followed by four other operas. His depression, however, continued unabated. 'I have always carried a big bag of melancholy

Portrait of Giacomo Puccini (1858-1924), taken in his last year of life (From: G. Böhme, Medical Portraits, vol. 2).

with me,' he wrote in November 1920. His physical health was threatened in all those years by his excessive nicotine consumption. In 1924 he became aware of a disorder of the windpipe which, after closer examination, appeared to be a larynx carcinoma. Puccini died several months later of this disease, before he was able to present his last great work, *Turandot*, to the public.

Depression and music in the twentieth century

Despite all sorts of discussions in the thirties and forties about the totally altered and still changing place of music in modern society, in which music has become a common property as a result of inventions such as the gramophone and radio, and after many intensive debates about their primarily negative effect on the therapeutic use of music in psychiatry, new perspectives nevertheless seemed to open up for music therapy after the Second World War. Particularly in the United States, where music therapy had a primarily social-psychoanalytical orientation, this method of treatment met with great interest. A milestone was the founding of the American *National Association for Music Therapy* in 1950.

In Europe the revived interest was divided into various different clinical-empirical schools, each of them representing an own direction from a wide spectrum of music-therapeutic movements: from philosophic-metaphysical to purely neurophysiological. The Swedish or depth-psychological school of Aleks Pontvic (*Der tönende Mensch. Psychorhytmie als gehörseelische Erziehung*, 1962) [The sounding human being. Psychorhythmics as auditory-psychological training] belonged to the metaphysical current, as did of course the anthroposophic, primarily therapy-oriented school of Rudolf Steiner (1861-1925). The early sixties also saw the emergence of the Viennese school (Koffer-Ullrich) which actually pursued the theory of the proportioned order according to Pythagoras. Lastly, there was a Marxist-oriented movement (Christoph Schwabe) which presented itself in Leipzig and based its thoughts on the conviction that music was an aesthetic form of communication and therefore constituted a permanent element of human behaviour.

Music therapy is presently defined as 'a diagnosis-specific method of treatment in psychotherapy which, adjusted to psychopathological requirements, receptively and actively applies the specific communication medium, music, in order to obtain therapeutic effects in the treatment of neuroses, psychosomatic disorders, psychoses and neuropsychiatric illnesses' (Simon 1975). The conclusion that depressive patients in particular would benefit from these new forms of music therapy (Bock 1975) proves once again that the thought of a 'circulus therapiae', of the alternating flourishing and decline of empirically substantiated, but not 'scientifically' explainable methods of treatment, also in the history of therapy for depressive disorders, is an established part of the historical development.

Bibliography

General

G. Bandmann, *Melancholie und Music. Iconographische Studien*, Köln and Opladen: Westdeutscher Verlag, 1960.

L. Bock, 'Musiktherapie und Zeiterleben in der Depression', in: Harrer, *Grundlagen der Musiktherapie und Musikpsychologie*, pp. 231-236.

G. Böhme, *Medizinische Porträts berühmter Komponisten*, Stuttgart-New York: Gustav Fischer, 1979 (vol. I) and Stuttgart-New York: G. Fischer and Kassel-Basel: G. Bärenreiter, 1987 (vol. II).

P.J. Buchoz, 'Nouvelle méthode de guérir la mélancholie par la Musique', in: Marquet, *Nouvelle Méthode facile et curieuse*, pp. 174-202.

G. Harrer (ed.), *Grundlagen der Musiktherapie und Musikpsychologie*, Stuttgart: G. Fischer, 1975.

J. Henkemans, *Aspecten van de sublimatie, haar stoornissen en de therapie hiervan*, 1981 (Thesis Amsterdam University).

S.E. Henschen, 'On the function of the right hemisphere of the brain in relation to the left in speech, music and calculation', *Brain* 49 (1926), pp. 110-126.

Ch. Kohler, *Musiktherapie. Theorie und Methodik*, Jena: G. Fischer Verlag, 1971.

W.F. Kümmel, *Musik und Medizin. Ihre Wechselbeziehungen in Theorie und Praxis von 800 until 1800*, Freiburg/Munich: Verlag Karl Aber, 1977 (esp. pp. 281-306).

W. Lange-Eichbaum and W. Kurth, *Genie, Irrsinn und Ruhm. Genie-Mythus und Pathographie des Genies*, Munich-Basel: E. Reinhardt Verlag, 1967 (6th printing).

E. Lesky, 'Van Swietens Hypochondrie. Zur Berufskrankheit der Gelehrten und zur Musiktherapie', *Clio Medica* 8 (1973) pp. 171-190.

(M.)F.N. Marquet, *Nouvelle Méthode facile et curieuse, pour connoitre le pouls par les notes de la Musique. Seconde Edition, Augmentée... par M. Pierre-Joseph Buchoz*, Amsterdam-Paris: Didot, 1769.

H.J. Möller, 'Psychotherapeutische Aspekte in der Musikanschauung der Jahrtausende', in: Revers, *Neue Wege der Musiktherapie*, pp. 53-160.

H. de la Motte-Haber, *Handbuch der Musikpsychologie*, Laaber: Laaber-Verlag, 1985.

Aleks Pontvik, *Grundgedanken zur psychologischen Heilwirkung der Musik*, Zurich, 1948.

A. Pontvik, *Der tönende Mensch. Psychorhytmie als gehörseelische Erziehung*, Zurich-Stuttgart: Rascher Verlag, 1962.

J.Chr. Reil, *Rhapsodieen über die Anwendung der psychischen Curmethode auf Geisteszerrüttungen*, Halle: Curtschen Buchhandlung, 1803.

J.W. Revers et al. (ed.), *Neue Wege der Musiktherapie. Grundzüge einer alten und neuen Heilmethode*, Düsseldorf, 1974.

J. Schumacher, 'Musik als Heilfaktor bei den Pythagoreern im Licht ihrer naturphilosophischen Anschauungen' in: Teirich, *Musik in der Medizin*, pp. 1-16.

Chr. Schwabe, 'Die Methodik der Musiktherapie und deren theoretische Grundlagen. Versuch einer Konzeption', in: Harrer, *Grundlagen der Musiktherapie und Musikpsychologie*, pp. 143-164.

W.C.M. Simon, 'Abriß einer Geschichte der Musiktherapie', in: Harrer, *Grundlagen der Musiktherapie und Musikpsychologie*, pp. 135-142.

J. Starobinski, *Geschichte der Melancholiebehandlung von den Anfängen bis 1900*, Basel: J.R. Geigy, 1960.

H.R. Teirich (ed.), *Musik in der Medizin. Beiträge zur Musiktherapie*, Stuttgart: Verlag G. Fischer, 1958.

Saul and David

W. Kümmel, 'Melancholie und die Macht der Musik. Die Krankheit König Sauls in der historischen Diskussion, *Medizinhistorisches Journal* 4 (1969), pp. 189-209.

S.S. Levin, *Adam's Rib. Essays on Biblical Medicine*, California: Geron-X, 1970.

G. Rosen, 'Is Saul also among the Prophets?', *Gesnerus* 23 (1966), pp. 132-146.

Hugo van der Goes

Dupré and Devaux, 'La mélancholie du peintre Hugo Vandergoes', *Nouvelle Iconographie de la Salpêtrière*, Sept./Oct. (1910) and *Journal de Neurologie* 16 (1911), pp. 21-27.

Ch. Grimbert, 'La mélothérapie dans l'antiquité et son application à la mélancolie du peintre Hugo van der Goes (1420-1482)', *Bulletin de la Societé française d'Histoire de la Médicine* 18 (1924), pp. 149-152.

H.G. Sander, 'Beiträge zur Biographie Hugo van der Goes', *Repertorium Kunstwissenschaften* 35 (1912), pp. 519-545.

J. Stellingwerff, *Werkelijkheid en grondmotief bij Vincent Willem van Gogh*, Amsterdam: Swets and Zeitlinger, 1959.

F. Winkler, *Das Werk des Hugo van der Goes*, Berlin: Walter de Gruyter and Co., 1964.

Carlo Broschi Farinelli

Cabanès, *Le Mal Héréditaire. Les Bourbons d'Espagne*, Paris: A. Michel, no year.

F. Haböck, *Die Gesangkunst der Kastraten. Erster Notenband: A. Die Kunst des Cavaliere Carlo Broschi Farinelli, B. Farinellis berühmte Arien. Eine Stimmungsbiographie in Beispielen*, Vienna: Universal-Edition, 1923.

Wolfgang Amadeus Mozart

H. Abert, W.A. Mozart, Leipzig: Breitkopf, 1955-1956 (7th printing).

C. Bär, *Mozart. Krankheit-Tod-Begräbnis*, Salzburg: Bärenreiter, 1966.

P.J. Davies, 'Mozart's illnesses and death', *Journal of the Royal Society of Medicine* 76 (1983), pp. 776-785.

J.H. Eibl, *Mozart. Briefe und Aufzeichnungen*, Kassel-Basel: Bärenreiter, 1971-1975.

A. Hutchings, *Mozart de musicus*; and idem, *Mozart de mens*, Baarn: Phonogram, 1977 (2 vols.).

F. Reichsman, 'Life experiences and creativity of great composers: a psychosomaticist's view', *Psychosomatic Medicine* 43 (1981), pp. 291-300.

Ludwig van Beethoven

A.E. Caldwell, 'La Malinconia: Final Movement of Beethoven's Quartet Op. 18, No. 6 – A Musical Account of Manic Depressive States', *Journal of the American Medical Women's Association* 27 (1972), pp. 241-248.

G.R. Marek, *Beethoven. Biography of a Genius*, New York: Funk and Wagnalls, 1970.

A. Schindler, *Biographie von Ludwig van Beethoven*, Münster: Aschendorff, 1840 (2nd enlarged edition, 1845).

E. and R. Sterba, *Beethoven and his Nephew. A Psychoanalytic Study of their Relationship*, New York: Pantheon, 1954.

A.W. Thayer, *The life of Ludwig van Beethoven*, Carbondale: Southern Illinois University Press, 1960 (reprint edition 1921), edited by Elliot Forbes.

E. Valentin, *Die schönsten Beethovenbriefe*, Munich-Vienna: Langen-Müller, 1973.

A 19th century quartet: Rossini, Schumann, Tchaikovsky and Puccini

Aside from G. Böhme, *Medizinische Porträts berühmter Komponisten*:

M. Carner, *Puccini. A Critical Biography*, London: G. Duckworth, 1958.

F.H. Franken, *Krankheit und Tod großer Komponisten*, Baden-Baden etc.: Verlag Gerhard Witzstrock, 1979.

J. Marx, *Gioacchino Rossini. Ausgewählte Briefe. Mit einer biographischen Skizze*, Berlin-Vienna-Leipzig: P. Zsolnay Verlag, 1947.

P.F. Ostwald, *Schumann: Music and Madness*, London: Victor Gollancz, 1985.

F. Thiess, *Puccini. Versuch einer Psychologie seiner Musik*, Berlin-Vienna-Leipzig: P. Zsolnay Verlag, 1947.

H. Weinstock, *Rossini: a biography*, New York: A.A. Knopf, 1968.